HERE IS THE SWEET HAND

francine j. harris

FARRAR STRAUS GIROUX

here
is the
sweet
hand

NEW YORK

Farrar, Straus and Giroux

120 Broadway, New York 10271

Copyright © 2020 by francine j. harris

All rights reserved

Printed in the United States of America

First edition, 2020

Library of Congress Cataloging-in-Publication Data

Names: Harris, Francine J., author.

Title: Here is the sweet hand : poems / francine j. harris.

Description: First edition. | New York : Farrar, Straus and Giroux, 2020. |
   Includes bibliographical references. | Summary: "A new collection
   of poems from the author of *allegiance*" —Provided by publisher.

Identifiers: LCCN 2020012281 | ISBN 9780374168841 (hardcover)

Subjects: LCGFT: Poetry.

Classification: LCC PS3608.A78284 H47 2020 | DDC 811/.6—dc23

LC record available at https://lccn.loc.gov/2020012281

Our books may be purchased in bulk for promotional,
educational, or business use. Please contact your local
bookseller or the Macmillan Corporate and Premium
Sales Department at 1-800-221-7945, extension 5442, or by
e-mail at MacmillanSpecialMarkets@macmillan.com.

www.fsgbooks.com

www.twitter.com/fsgbooks

www.facebook.com/fsgbooks

10 9 8 7 6 5 4 3 2 1

It is not only about "us"; it is also about me and you. Just the two of us.

—Toni Morrison

If no one and I speak in the fire we can turn our backs on
leaders, and all but that which concerns us, our loss.

—Alice Notley

CONTENTS

i.

ii.

i.

Versal

The wood is not a negro with tree in the farm-split sand
for almighty, not a road to bend over,
not a lakeside, or sideways log stump, not
a sidelong, not a strangler clutch

or fruiting body of fungus. The warn
of wood is not hiding in bark, in deer suit,
or elk piss musk, not in camouflage. Not
a snowshoe a negro, not a cowhide stripped

or oversprawl. The tree is not a loner type, not
a sleeper cell, not a jumpy trigger.
The foliage low hangs a lake I like, an ice cave
shot, a hit tide, frozen in place.

And a black girl is standing on it, over a river rocking.
Sidebank isn't thug among us, not
a rush gang, not a flower snatched from sidewalks,
which isn't breaking in root. Nothing

for jewels, isn't watching through windows. The black meadow
isn't sniper squatting, cheapening the field reek,

eyesore cattail driving down
the sound of stream driveby. The wood

is an eager, a Negus among us, a runner like eagle,
a brown sighting, root system gathered in growl
of curl, of amassed vein feed. Say it with us.
The wood is a falcon, a clean stretch of might.

The dark bark is humming. Night stretched.
A reserve is craning in its path glow, pitch fall.
Matted grass atrament, blowing night
like long husk. and a black girl is standing in it.

Reflections in a Pool of Hair

You have been standing in a pool of your own hair.
You rub the hair into dirt and pick out crows you'd like to lift it away.

You take off your socks.
Hand to eyes to block the sun, you look
      for someone who looks like you.

You see men in retro glasses, you see men behind retrofitted glass
and men on black bikes and women with small
piercings in their sharp noses and you see their bad silver nail polish, you've got
bad silver nail polish

and everyone wheezes. You wheeze
and the small gay men at the bar spend sunset
tuning *American Idol* onto two screens.

They talk like bar glass. In their gravel, they vote singers.

There is a tingle at the back of your throat that holds the phone on hold
and thinks the words

Obama.

Obama wants to be a palindrome.

You catch yourself in a plate glass window, you catch yourself

in the neighbor's glass plate, you catch yourself

wondering if you look like your hair

in their windows. They put away things

as soon as you ask about them.

The Meek

It's Election Day. It's the finest day in history. The air
is crisp and the tone is full of hope. My party is weighing in early.
There are victory flags in the sky. And the whole morning I am haunted
by the memory of a lover who at the end of everything
told me I had no ass.

Limulus Polyphemus

"Who you looking at?"

—Fred Moten

In class, I stared because of the blood going blue.
the chalk that coated our fingerly teeth.
the way we lapped each other (on the shore
where the flowering). I gave away

our location. Smacked my lips in the coat closet.
sucked at her teeth. We, on all eights, we had magical
innards. Coagulated ground germ. We stood in the torture lights.

Sandy liked to say in those moments: *What the fuck
you looking at,* in a rasp. her smooth neck of coal coast.
in the shells they brought in. Her, whose voice I can still hear.
We sat still at that. In carapace, in book gill. The UV light
of her face in my face. We dodge at first, then the stainless plunge.

I am overhear. Wanting you to sense in me.
the medicinal leak. the thick abating. If they
are bacteria, so coalesce. The beginning
world is in you. The old story. Did I ever get
the pleasure of your fist. Did you kick at me

custodially. Knock around a bean in my skull.
So rattle, Rattler. Mimic the scorpion. Head
caved in. rolling to a crab-hard squint.

Or was it mouth spray. cover story. Whatever we bled out
was given to white men for research before they kicked us
back to sea. half faint. half apocalypse. Beauty, Blue.
It was hideous what we gnarled into house. under our hard shell.
stabbed at and raked over. I was nothing but eyes. a million
ommatidia, plus a pair of median desires to sense out. to sea.
If we could fuck in the open, on the wide-open shore. black
sand. Would I be the dead woman whose back she clung to.

Ask me now and I would say

I caught my hair on fire in a fistfight. We had
decorative words. I took up

tree lights in her mouth and though it was summer.
We lit up bits of river like we picked switch.

The cockeyed girl snatched off my wigs at the nape.
It was all kinds of monstrous.

We were all on the ground like gravel and glass.
We splattered each other all dusk after campfire snack.

Then she beef up, while I sat monkey-faced
and open-headed and someone in another cabin bet chicken strips on our
    appetite.

Someone in those moments is sure to get scratched.

She grew out her nails for it.
I lit her up in the dark. In this retelling, we both spit out

hunks of each other on the bathroom lawn where raccoons ditch.
In this version, no one succumb. No freeze on a narrative

and all explain away bully by her dark-skinned cheek.
In this retelling, I get beneath her

in the greased grass. I watch the star
in her eye and we

roll over it. We unbridle that shit.

What Milkman Leaps For

The sugar wings of a myth, a guiltless grandfather, a man with no
dark side, a gelatinous memory that feels pretty good, three hundred
dollar shoes feel right, alright. Like wings look good on in the mirror,

handmade so you could star in a play with 'em. or host a garden party
in 'em. So you could dim the lights and burn myrrh, tank it to the hallways
where guests linger perusing installations of you in your wings. Where you

could fly off but all flights up and leave someone. All the rebels who
choose flock over children at home. The warrior who thinks a good fight
and whose family sits home practicing the epitaph. Back at Pilate's, she

scratches out hair and her good looks. The bedridden turns to cough
in the absence of a hero. Her gold miner, her reborn takes to air
to transcend the what. the dark marks on the wall. Awakened, it ain't

easy as it lifts. It can take up the outside, let alone it has to be
a man at all. Let's skip that part, and say it can walk over heavy shoes,
over bear-eaten bodies. Be the one to fly the flight homeward,

with myths thick enough to drag river, to turn up bodies, to unrest
the dead with their socks on, who still reek of corn whiskey, who still
smell of many masters' breath. And better yet, who still fingerprint

gunpowder, or worse, who still like little girls. Oh, what Milkman
steps off into. The air full of no one you can't consistently count on.

(Let's try again) whose fault it all is. He mean: No one who show up for
nothing you aren't celebrating. No one to bounce you on birthday knees
or bounce birthday checks. No one not high enough to talk to when

school is out, it's all myth with its skin lightened, with its orderly shoes.
He no longer has to pinpoint balance; it has perched itself in the wreck
of nesty hair clumped at bedside. He no longer has to be the unsettled,

the conquered, the harvest. He takes to the air to tribe in good grace,
to stake the ground, to clan. He puts on wings and throws open the doors
to faceless partygoers. He rounds up all the sexy people, calls them all

fam, drops brown liquor to their mouths and let's not even speak
of rebellion. The heroes do their rounds. In troops they brush.
They take targets from a distance, just the four or fifteen of them.

Just the crew. The families back home, taking out little bits
of their skin. For this point, this nation. One less song
so tomorrow is the fight in a cave and milk walking out.

Abortion

One warm and summer evening, she has rubbed the pulp
of banana between her fingers and pushed it around
the rim of a clear and heavy vase, and showed
me how to hold it tight, almost to shatter
but just enough to keep the slippery flame
beneath her, the thick stink of candle lit
and placed beneath her bulge white gown, this
white woman hangs, living, from a noose
and holds the rope firmly in her own grip
which is like,
             and unlike
silhouette tapestries Kara Walker made
of a little girl who was hanged outside
a burning orphanage, one warm night
in 1863, in retaliation
for jobs some theory of negro would take from
white Irish workers should the draft
free slaves and allow them into factories, which
is the sense she does not want to grow inside
herself from her blond and lover's touch, his lips
a kind of popped, soft, plump over
the wick and fire, which I center beneath her open

legs and as soon as the heat is ready and lifts, and
as soon as he holds her hips in place and she holds
the hang in place and I hold the urn in place,

we look. Which she, of course, can't see. that almost kiss.

Against Storm, Against Glib Thunder

When I was the red umbrella, her lover, I made a precision of hoist.
We understood stairs, my girl. We waited the hall, its curse, 'til the sky
undid clouds, uncoiled in loose slip of rain and I waited for the first
hushed sun to pattern after a harp above her, a sure sign of song as tarp,
a sun against patter, against storm, against glib thunder rumble, against
chatter, we rubbed.

When I was the red umbrella, her lover, I made a precision of hoist and
sold metal as a system of limb, as a static frigate to keep red gular pouch
above her, so she might know love as cover, such awkward inflation
and swarm below her that she might know the egg of warmth, a nest of
articulating spread. without rust. without the gait of heavy chest to lift
off her in the sun.

When I was the red umbrella, her love, I made a precision of hoist
among her. I stood down when she had an army of metals, when she
claimed command, armed with finches, mad with rain. I would never
invade any cover for shelter. I never put her country at thirst. I wanted
to leave ranks loved, or wet, depending on the map on which artillery
she wanted posed. I snapped, whenever. whenever she snapped.

When I was the red umbrella, her love, I made a precision of hoist.

and got so good you couldn't see me erect. Prone I arched, like

the snake of a vine, the bank of a tree limb. I gathered moisture from air

and I put buds in her black wrath of hair. I wanted all bees to swim us,

roped through breeze, our spiny ribs licked into a sway of combs they

stung to. I wanted us open. so she could see me drape.

She is what I undo

and rely and muster.

and battle the curve   of reserve and sake for.

She is how I groan, midday. what lapse unnoon. how

the traipse of mirror, if mirrors were dumb.

I must uncolor the cum I from within her. redone.

re-myrrh. Remembered of hiss, and tucked

kiss is how I slip. I mention hips. I mention *brun*.

I mention the tackle of talon in grass, the noon's

undoing. I beg her stirrup. and what a knot of horse,

we don. We dun in moon. We flock up rust and bury

her blouse and miss river. miss the humps below

tums of belly flower. Mostly, murder, she slumps

      a fit of jelly and makeup, a stage of ragged

and plunder, whatever that fit of sun and petal fetter is.

Stuff, she says. and stuffs

in tongue full. gumful. *There is no western this dumb*

in downing. this dung swell of shadow's day,

I tell her. That's what I tell her. She doesn't
even brush   my shoulder when we fold
                    into tupelo   mud.

The fat of the fog hovers over

a man who sits inside his canoe, beached at the shore. He sits inside it
swaying. The thick is so close, only a few
ducks swim, visible. The lake itself has vanished. Behind me
traffic lights like helium as evening

rolls forward and I wave. Because one figure is sketched
inside the steam of another and down
the beach, geese lift. A couple on a bench
scatter inside their own gray mist. Earlier

it was clear and warm. I was on the phone
for hours with a woman I keep getting it wrong with.
I tried telling her which fruit I cut too early. The hard green
pulp of avocado that won't yield its pit. That I bike

out of breath in warm months, and how empty the dark
buildings in the city, glass on the floor. What you could hear
crunch and echo like voice, but that's a story
she knows. Everybody knows it. Instead, I tell her

I can't help but wait. In the fog, that cruelty
waves back from his boat. He gets out and wraps

its skin like an ankle inside a ballerina's slipper. He docks it on a squat dolly. He walks toward me and drags

the limp thing through the sand.

Rabbit

for Tarfia and Fita

The rabbit has a funny set of tools. He jumps.
or kicks. muffled and punching up. In pose
the rabbit knows, each side of his face to whom.
he should belong. He hobbles and eyes. This
is the dumb allegiance. This bunny, even dry and fluff
is aware, be vicious. will bite down your finger stalk.
will nick you good in the cheery web of your palm.
Those claws are good for traction. and defense.
This bunny, forgive him. There is no ease. His lack
of neck is all the senses about a stillness.
stuck in a calm. until household numbers upend
his floor. until the family upsets the nest
and traipses off. Then stuck in a bunny panic.

We each stab at gratitude. In our nubbing, none
of us do well. We jump. We kangaroo. We soft seeming,
scatter and gnaw. Maybe the only way forward
is to sleep all day. one eye open. under the sink.
Like the rabbit, we could sit in our shit.
chew at the leaf of others' dinner. Make
of each tile on the floor a good spot to piss. No,

it doesn't get much better. And like the rabbit
we do not jump well from heights. We linger the dark
until it is safe to come out. to offer a nose.
a cheek for touch. the top of a crown. Nothing
makes us happier than another rabbit.

Here is the sweet hand you
always turn back on yourself

and hold where the ear goes and try to hear what you need to hear.
the way it was put. A bird went to the phone pole and knocked a
hundred times, and here I was looking for a hammer all along

to knock back.

All the tools are crushed. I swear to them I only make sense
between periods. Translation comes awfully late. And if the woodpecker
got out of control, caught up in a pole rung, for example. well, my
forehead. I am well pecked

and out of excuse. There is nothing to sit on. or quit under. or curse out.
or thump with my knuckle. There is a malady of separate
conversations converged under the woodpecker's knockknock.

He is much louder than usual. And somewhere, I have already

fucked off forgiveness and died in the grass. And somewhere there is
a hand. I ought to use it to bury this pecked-out eyeball with a mallet
and a horseshoe. or a mortar and pestle. And I ought to stop saying

I can't hear people when all I ever hear is this steady knock.

Language works over information . . .

Being alone affects the canvas under language. its hold. its black
through the window. the cloth behind the feud. And by the way

it is a feud. a battle about battling. a conflict over
agreement. Language works over information.
Someone in the audience says:
>   *You mean works over, like in a fight. Like a war.*

The author hadn't thought of this. says:
>   *Well . . . yes.*
The woman sits back in her seat. As in

takes over. as in takes a bullet to a statistic's brain.
pulls along generalities in a dead body wagon.
plants landmines in long redundancies. red herring.
does the editing in hubs of triage. This

the living, barely breathing language. This
the language with no hope for a new organ. Now this
over here language could be saved, if only

we had enough oxygen. There is no oxygen. But here,
this language only needs a suture for its passive voice.
a simple interrupted stitch for its drone-on spiel. Language takes
information by its hair and rides it

nighttime. It is hardly soft on the reins. is not some given space
where soft falls. This is always responding in defense
of the gallop. in defense of the whip on the croup.
Dying is something you have to do on purpose,
in words. Like it or not, it's some bloodsporter wearing a strip of burlap
  on its forehead.
It's a spelled-out gun nut throwing itself on the enemy's sandbag daggers.
You'd think you could say *Fuck 'em, let 'em think what they want to think.*
The woman in the audience uncrosses her legs.
and her arm goes up.
        So really language has a bone to pick with information.

The author hadn't thought of this. says
        Well . . . maybe.

But what about the average mark. Language
is typical. It only sticks upon repetition.
upon trend. when repeated. When repeated
the lone voice isn't always the one winning over information. Just ask
a middle schooler why the poet wrote the poem.
        'Cause she crazy.
The lone voice could be mistaken. Everybody says so.

The lonely voice is lonely. Listens for someone in the kitchen
to break something. Thinks: It could be worse. It could be
an ambient tape for the ones who are left behind. artificially domestic.

plates clinking. bags being emptied. the floor being swept. breath in a room.

II.

For the absence of
language, there is more than one side.
Somebody hold me once, like you once held me.
unassuming. Don't work over me. not yet. Don't
try to win everything. not yet. Don't already be lost. a foregone
tendency. a gimmick. Don't already
give up. believe in will. (I'll fight you for it.) *(not yet)*
wrestle with it. (I'll fight you for it.) Stay.

I'll believe it is more than anomaly, if that helps.
Even an anomaly can catch on. if repeated. or.
repeated. could become a trend. Language works
over information. or. works underneath it. Like
a camp. like that which does not bother to hide its fabrication.
To work. that which is the dirt earth housing the explosion
underneath itself.

You could say language is really
trying to kill information.

for the reduction of dead space, the over and over again suture.
That which is blown apart. before it takes place.
That wound bleeding open. that
limb soaking the ground. that tongue parting
the lips. a heat traveling through rooms:

Only a trained professional can gather the air with
decision. can work with this much absent language. The medic
begins to feel for the explosion. presses for, below the ground. below
the housing of blood and. the horizontal mattress suture. heat spells:

This one to an open bed.

Heat says:

This one (I'm afraid) is gone.

Heat moves the medic closer to some thumping heart lay apart.
chest blown. mouth tongue ripped out. chest gaping,
organ soaking the ground.

So language has nothing to lose
compared to information.

The medic leans forward. The author hadn't thought about this: says
Well . . . no.
But the eyes are still fluttering. under information.
a kind of anomaly. Still working. still trying to move; lone voice

to trend. To live above the intelligence. the flash. In the form
of language. or below information, as in. final report. Below, as a sense
of heat. Heat moves the medic's hand, says:

This one might make. it. stands to stutter, something.

Stitch up the heart.

I love you	2	3	4
I love you	2	3	4
I love you	2	3	4
I love you	2	3	4
I love you	2	3	4
I love you	2	3	4
I love you	2	3	4
I love you			

Junebug

Fat thing with no direction but
occasional flap. emerged from the sofa where

your voice is warm. I take the fat of it
home with me and lose it between

the cushions. I can't
imagine you any thinner if it's revolution

you want, I'm gunless like a thing with wings.
see-through and stuck with resin

sacs. All night I put up your
bad plans on a map. Your hands

go sideways, like a diagonal gnat
of blankets. Have you ever as a grown

woman touched a photo of a grown woman
and let it fall crooked beneath

you and sat with the downfall, down
where you exaggerated movements to get it

off the ground, her waistline impossible. your fingers long
and summery, it won't stay still until I tell you. Which is funny you say

since it's the silliest thing going as her breasts slip
below her shirt. It's summer after all on the train tracks, in her

photographs she has on the best
lip gloss I've ever noticed. Maybe now that I have

stopped flailing my arms and throwing
myself against the walls.

barycenter

i was the i-want-you. i was the hungry at girl and girl glass.

and everything changed when the brown dwarf saw its star food.

everything changed when the hungry reached in where its hand could

would naturally reach. i was that one. that implosion who would be

in the would-be window. who would reach the i-want-you through

the echo explosion, be damned. i was the two-body problem.

your lids would reflect a flashback. we would be twin-year lens

closest to red suns. would match your would-be lip. so

i would be your sister, then. since you put it that way.

touching you where it would be normal, then. i was

would-be food and it *would* take place in a breath. a

second star. where the i-want-you *would* be gases

only a scope could reach. then, of course you would have

to look. and it would change everything. now i am the

would-be. the it-then, the heat hunger changed to light. hydrogen

double-talked into spitting cloud. it would be food to a hungry.

and it would take a million to hear you because it would be spinning winter.

your eyes would get hoarse in the damp light. because i love brown

fallout and so of course, your voice would muffle underweight and you would keep

saying *molecule*—one after the other like that, and they would make up this

named debris. and of course you would hate that. the hunger and orbit and wobble.

because they would be familiar then too, of course. why i hated yours too. so it makes sense i would say it easier. because firstborn, maybe, that

protostar. a potential for light. you would hate that in your *sister*.

naturally. we would abort plans and stain eyelids. in a would-be dust

blood letter for what marks left in the sky and it would

bludgeon the drift. your heavy throat would make those gases

tangle like cord. i was forever the see-it-all before

it happened. so the telescope. i would smell choke and

you would map it out. hungry for familiar light

our separate births would watch all familiar people die

like this, then.

destined, since you say so. doomed not to fall into one another's

pitch of family grave. lips still aflame. you would watch me

orphan. mouth out *mother* and sing me *tralala.* it would hurt my ears.

you would be hungerfood. so, of course,

sputtering,

i would see those other stars fall out

into gray silt, and i would perch on your aching spine.   i would *halala*

and you would hear it all wrong. and you would say *youfuckingtalktoomuch.* and, yes, i

of course glutton, now that

you mention it. i guess we would windowbreak each other in less than perfect

sibling/sorrytheblood. that

i would be your hungry star-sister. and naturally we would dwarf to each spin, a fail

so it makes sense.

Single Lines Looking Forward
or One Monostich Past 45

The joke is orange. Which has never been funny.

For a while, I didn't sleep on my bright side.

Many airplanes make it through sky.

The joke is present: dented and devil.

For a while, yellow spots on the wall.

Obama on water skis, the hair in his armpits, free.

I thought the CIA was operative.

Across the alley, a woman named Mildred.

Above the clouds in a plane, a waistline of sliced white.

I don't sound like TED Talk, or smart prose on Facebook.

These clouds are not God.

I keep thinking about Coltrane; how little he talked.

This is so little, I give so little.

Sometimes when I say something to white people, they say, "I'm sorry?"

During Vietnam, Bob Kaufman stopped talking.

The CIA was very good at killing Panthers.

Mildred in a housecoat, calling across the fence, over her yard.

If I were grading this, I'd be muttering curses.

The joke is a color. A color for prison.

Is it me, or is the sentence, as structure, arrogant.

All snow, in here, this writing, departure.

All miles are valuable. All extension. All stretch.

I savor the air with both fingers, and tongue.

Mildred asks about the beats coming from my car.

I forgot to bring the poem comparing you to a garden.

Someone tell me what to say to my senators.

No one smokes here; in the rain, I duck away and smell piss.

I thought the CIA was. the constitution.

I feel like he left us, for water skis, for kitesurfing.

The sun will not always be so gracious.

From the garden poem, one line stands out.

Frank Ocean's "Nights" is a study in the monostich.

Pace is not breathing, on and off. off.

Mildred never heard of Jneiro Jarel.

I'm afraid one day I'll find myself remembering this air.

The last time I saw my mother, she begged for fried chicken.

My father still sitting there upright, a little high.

Melissa McCarthy could get it.

Sometimes, I forget how to touch.

In a parking garage, I wait for the toothache.

I watch what I say all the time now.

She said she loved my touch; she used the word *love*.

In 1984, I'd never been in the sky.

My mother walked a laundry cart a mile a day for groceries.

Betsy DeVos is confirmed, with a broken tie.

Mildred's five goes way up, and my five reaches.

Anise Swallowtail, Molting

He says *papillon* and you want to take
his word for it. The thorax is missing its yellow wing.

What do you say when that happens. *Muer.* he says.
He says you thought it meant woman. But no,
he says, and his chin. The slender proboscis drinks nectar.

Like a straw, you say. Yes, he says. Has one ever fallen
on your sweat in summer. won't always get
enough salt, from flower. The ocean, you think.
Alive, he says,

they are hidden in tree limbs, mimic the bark. You think:
Yeah, but the trees here are rotten and burned.
and it looks like a moth, torn. Others,
he says, sniff the air for stem.

You want to ask: How many fingers
to tear up the butterfly. But you know he'll say if
they are only children, it does not count.
You would smoke from the wingtip

and flame the wing. You say the sun is shot here.

Everyone's on edge. He says any excuse, you'd trap
butterflies in tupperware and ask strangers
dumb questions like:

What do you call it when a dead thing's wing comes off?
You say you'd tell someone anyway. You say you'd get
the crying over with. If it was a little girl in dirt,
touch her sun-edged hair.

Tender, he says, what doesn't know how to treat
limb's fruit. The same to you. You want the one
in the bowl who has lost her articulated flutter. To stand
up to the claws. To fight back. He says,

You'd still snuff it out. Ask anyone. You say:
Your French words make me feel bad. You
should ask if he means it. if he means *papillon* you.
Is he thinking of a dead one. one

that smells of fennel. What would he have called it
when he was a boy in the dirt. tearing wings in the dirt.
He says, well then. Then, who do we blame.

ii.

I won't beg.

I have before. I took off a skin. I put it
in paint. I tried to make it better with me
than doing it alone. I won't fall off. The escape
is shaky. It looks out over boys driving
cars with toy black remotes. They are actually
men. They are men in the wide zoom of street.
Engine makes them hug. They trade the remotes
loud over bright green skins. I won't panic.
The plastic so fat and wide, it can get in a lane.
It can do a 180. I won't sick. It's a lump
in the throat. When the dirt bikes head out in a rip
to twilight, they hop off. I won't jump. As they tilt
a ruddy thing and hand it over to the next.
The chest is sore, right there. I won't beg. The blast
of generators spits out dirty white light.
A white man on the train with enormous eyes put
his fingers in the shape of a gun and shot another
white man twice, in the face. Before he deboarded
he said fuck white supremacy, *you're all*
gonna pay and I won't body. I won't block.
I am putting the tip of his finger to my forehead. I won't

yank. When I open the door, I am the whole
brick wall. Its impossible angle. I am looking out
the window at night against the glare of light.
I can only see the men who ground in voices.

Sonata in F Minor, K.183: Allegro

[Domenico Scarlatti, Daria van den Bercken]

Car tires rush through and announce the rain. You can hear
the shuffling of someone street sweeping in the street.
The insistent men outside Stingray's, the cutoff lull
of ambulance testing siren, the women. who step in the street and yell
to anyone they loved once and it sounds like prelude if
     Scarlatti hadn't moved to Madrid

     would he have moved the notes diatonically as the rain falls up

a roof. ascends the scaffolding. It's impossible to read *The Street*
without seeing Mrs. Hedges on mine. leaning from a window on the ground
level of my building peering out under her red bandana considering
me as I lean my body over the rail and watch the men dressed
black and in gray I tell a man to stop peeing on my car and when
     he turns around. he is not surprised. He says

     he isn't peeing, he
is counting his money.

Concerto No. 2 in G Minor, Op. 8, RV 315 "L'estate": I. Allegro mà non molto

[Antonio Vivaldi, I Solisti Aquilani, Daniele Orlando]

Underneath generators, if you tune it out, it becomes
its own vow of subaural buzz. Something is generating.
Something lit and moving low to the ground. A hush in festival,
night and how the bus rows the street over stoplights. Picking up
speed, it rounds nothing. No men out tonight. No crickets even
if winter is suffering a heat on all the snow melted and slick
ice quickly black has slipped off into greasy gutters and dried though

at midnight, the orchestra loses it. Breaks out of its trap shell. its lounge
doors. its shivering cymbals, and howls a lost dog into the steady drop
night where beneath the window the squash leaves are still fat and
yellowing a sign of dormant or disaster why night baptizes every
utterance, quickly black and restless children are always out now
of earshot, the red priest of Venice is bowing so lightly you have
to listen at full volume and when the men bellow suddenly into
half empty streets at night, it wakes everyone. everyone at once.

Unaccompanied Cello Suite No. 4 in E-Flat Major, BWV 1010: IV. Sarabande

[Johann Sebastian Bach, Yo-Yo Ma]

The tension is in drag. the rug of hot winter rain. the droll swish tires.
One of the old men comes to dance three times a night on a Monday.
None of them sorry drizzle, rushing women, honking cab. The ones pass
who speak sometimes. The woman who brings her dog. the dog hushed.

When Carolina studied no violin and made no heirs, who stood beneath
her brothers' window; knockless. wet like mad white raven. little doused
blue blackbirds. little soggy clogs of fog harbinger. Who scuttled open
her womb to check for eggs, for ripe fallopian, for rich blood.

The hollow sound of his fingers, someone's fingers. low tread running
over wet ground. The silk ribbon bobbing. The arrogant breed.

Morceaux de fantaisie, Op. 3 No. 2: Prelude in C-Sharp Minor

[Sergey Rachmaninoff, Claire Huangci]

All these years later, the woman in front of Stingray's
is still calling the same man faggot for what he done
with her son and for twenty minutes she says
fuck you I'm out. In prelude, each descent is a final
way. a story at several endings. Beneath the note
she says: Let's go. which suggests a son.

When loneliness strikes, I remember we
were so night rapt our groins. felt earth our mouths
felt mated. No one could tell which was beneath
which dark settling to a final third. Dawn a movement.
arms and touch to climb from, and there it was. I cannot hear
her son say a word. He could be a child. He could be
a grown man. The man she screams is gone. The stars are out.

So is we thinking up new ways to fuck, or nah.

I got a lot to thrash. I don't mind sin in it.

I'mma make this point then I'mma snake. you off. I'd be lying
if I said this ain't. for thumb. All these snafus in my skin.
they turn you on. It's a lot of grope and mist unwraps the shit I'm on.

Herd, you hot; the type that you take bone to hog. Is we queening
when we need this done as song. I ain't lending ass for nothing; want
to see the drug I'm on. I'mma cock this throttle. you could give me
rain for God.

Would you dyke the day I wet. my tongue with tau.
You can hide your face until you most succumb. (I ain't spinning)
We can get the gist. and then we throat a song.
Come sic 'em. Stretch a bully on a prong.

I'm not the flight you crawl back up a star. But the way you wrap
around me's rather mob. Ain't nobody trying to save you.
May we get that langua. Got probably. knots
of other riches. on these labia. So we pushing scented nude,
had to paint a spot to save us. Shook fur in them glitches.
Gunned dirt to the air of night as fable.

We wrecking sexes' demirep. We trying to take the flitch as breath.
We trying to keep the spruce's debt. We trying to buck
their gender vends.   So. you going to fix it with these flatheads,
pearl or saw.   Scale me. Is you kneeling under sun with muscle
heat. or rah. Don't stay with loss. You know we're better
off. in a vug than a seal. hun. We can say it all:

Is we sealing bouts of honey, so raw.
Can we steely run. a grip that's flawed. Can I sling
another niche that's maw. Is you with the shits. or faux.
or craw. blue law. Would you high with a digger. rickshaw.
Would you die for the trick. cumshaw. Would you sigh for a bigger
macaw. bylaw. Hooke's law. Can you steely.
and flip. and claw. Can I bring another fitch, or nah.
Is you with the writs or gnaw, outlaw, scofflaw.

Would you high with a whip and bra.
Would you die with a vigor. geegaw.
Would you sigh for a swigger, pshaw. ringtaw.
World. make that class rap on young scholar spine.
You already go gunning for a song of whine. I could slide
into glycol.   With belly. Sweet serow's acinar gets messy.
Hurled. is you trucking tree. or suckling bee. or caw. Can I sling
another stich. Death has a sea slum seep braying. Two's a streak.
go move it or yaw. Quiz which me looking at me, who stick
in diff or flaw.

Who's a mag or pie glitch. stew raw tin. or thaw.

The way to do. Plot a side dish. skew fall in. and crawl.

You gon' make them eggs cheesy with them grits, or nah.

Then blue woo it right back. on this script and. voilà. ta-dah. ooolaw.

White People Eating White Food

You have not gone up against the plaster wall
with real plastic forks, lately, or ruined much dental

work with the metal studs hanging too fat and too quick
from your bleached Hanes, or let the overturn of your cock

puss. You lie in white sheets eating boxed potatoes
from a sectioned paper plate, watching reality's

skinny Texan as he speed-eats gummy worms, and slinkys
on commercial break, in a frame ad, then back to themed water

parks, with slip tubulature, like jellied condoms, like sweet
shower liners, such that the gaunt contestant stuffs

rough napkins inside his cheeks to keep. This is that kind
of room. It sounds like pink air conditioning. Such as the sort

is worn out. Who has white fun anymore. pink
fiberglass, insufflation. When girls ring

the downward door, you venge binge on their teeth. sucking

and hollering *fuck, come.* You complain of night terrors.
It's such faint panic. such wicker basket frantic while the sound

of Amazon's stick gets lost in the powdery mattress pads
like a Utah runway buffering white planes. You have large

salt bags bloating. a pillow between your legs, and a plated
grin. Which burrows with its white mint, digs. eyes like peeled

white carrot. In each window, white mayfly. dead
infest, stuck to the top of your lip until it splits.

I cleaned the house.

I moved the bookshelf from the radiator.
I put my brown things in boxes.
I threw away the cardboard.
I scrubbed the stove. and dried it with a black towel.
There is no more fray coming from under the area rug.
Broke a glass while doing it. and swept the glass. and wiped the glass.
I wiped the glass. And I looked for glass, stray in the break of the wood flooring.
Moved the couch and tried to find the glass heating its way into a wedge.
I imagined the foot on glass at some worst time: a phone interview.
a lovemaking. a day of the flu. I took a magnifying glass
to the glass. I thought there were strands of slivering into a splinter
so thin so thin you couldn't see. I imagined the glass elongating.
I imagined the glass cooling too quickly and snap. I threw away
the glove I used to look for the glass and wiped my knee with a white
towel. I shook the towel over the trash and wiped the floor
where I shook the towel and washed the towel and then washed
the sink where the towel stank. A woman came home and said
she was moving out. I put that dinner on a plate and slid it
beneath the glass bowl covering a salad on the second shelf
which upon its second onceover with a fork, has lost its verdant leaf.
In the bowl, through the glass, it's all trunk. The beet is sparse, the avocado
soggy and browning. Lettuce stalk is bitter and watery and hard.
In that distortion, I found a sharp tongue. And I knew I would stab it.
And I knew it would be so only delicious, to me.

Unlike my sister

I don't have children I won't bring to the city. or the city
beach. or the monkey bars. I don't curl my eyelashes in
the mirror with a whiteness. or a woman. or an iron bar.
I don't track sperm into cookie jars. or drag Budweiser
blankets to the pines. Or scowl when the priest crosses
my mother. I don't touch married men in their necks.
I am at my mother's funeral. and scissor off her hair.
and touch her fat lip.

I don't have any children who don't know their grandmother.
or old trees. or blood orange. I pull with both hands and both
teeth. and I wait until it's ready. I watch the sun go first.
I don't get high with mother's husbands. or blow smoke
in their dark mouths. or push tongue. I don't believe marrying
a white man will fix anything. or fork real good. or take it back.
That was kind of a lie. and I can say it was a lie. I don't use
pink makeup. I don't

like to lie. I don't have any children. who don't believe
in damage. who push metal up under cats' tails. or blow tire
smoke into married men's throats. I don't like funerals.
And so I keep them to myself. and so I touch them

with my teeth. In fact, I'm not the clammy beach. or the monkey bars. or a little girl's skirt hiked up. I don't show up in my sister's mirror. or on the grass in a glassy glitter. or in her spit.

Stand Up

The part to leave out is the part where you call and no one answers.
where the weather is choppy and everyone is sick. or off to a
wedding. or stuck in therapy. That part where they called and why
didn't you return their call. or the part where they don't return your
call. or the part where you don't call. or worried they will think
you're just like your old man. always wanting something. The part
where you don't go sniffing around after people. or the part where
you don't ask for it and get it anyway. Leave it in your mailbox. Shove
it in your coat pocket. Leave it on your desk from God's ways of
mystery. The part where people have to go. Have to get off the
phone now. Something burning. Something knocking. Something
needs to be let out. Be surprised who interrupts this story to tell you
about how they had a dream something like this would happen to
them. about the time they worried about it. The part you should
skip over is the part when you call and they say, *Well you know, just
call if you need anything.* and then they have to go. or they say, *You
know if you ever need to talk.* and then they have to go. or they say,
That must be hard. and then. Leave out the part where the
therapists interrupt you to tell you about their kids' graduation. or
about how well they've raised their well-adjusted kids. or the time
they had a dream something like that would happen to them. Skip
that part. Painting a sock. Stitching a recipe of yolk. Darning a list.
Talking to windows. to altars. to baby birds. dirt. the grass. Then the
cat talks back. Then the tea makes you a pot. Then you share it.

Tardigrade

I'm not saying close your eyes. I'm saying
don't look up from your food. your table.
your beer. The room is dark for a reason. keeps
everyone at a distance. keeps the redheaded
white boys: high and dry. keeps the bartender
where you can see him, your hands above the table.
The French, did you know, suspect dinner hands
of public pleasuring, down there. Americans don't
want your elbows. Americans put their elbows
on the table. A woman can cum and no one
would know. I'm doing it right now. I'm doing it
at the TVs in this wooden room. multiple televisions.
The sound is off in Traverse City. There are hoodies
behind the bar. Most of them are girlish. The ginger
says *chipotle*. He pronounces all the syllables.
The ginger has a beer belly. Is *ginger* a little racist.
How could a root be racist. I shave his fat body
with my bare hands, like a tardigrade. I shave it
down into my American bar curry soup. It lives
in my soup forever. It lives with its pig snout
in the napkins, on the fork, in my amber craft beer.
Little moss piglet. Little water bear. They say you can
see it. moving around near the wood. in your yard.

The Neighbor's Buddy Through the Window

Because the tube is turned to the window, the neighbor's buddy coughs
a cough of pigeons. a hack of grackle. a bird out the window. It's like

the neighbor's buddy on my ledge, smoking. The neighbor's chum
in the blinds, the eyes that peer, the eyes that open. propped

and sunglassed. a kind of smoking blackbird, an inveterate
tombirder. His leather wings are splayed. his rock in the cold.

He has one foot on ice porch and one foot wiggle.
one foot rockerbird. a one-foot band.

His cough is the cough of the myriad smoker, the murder of smoker.
There is quiver of murder. His cough is the cough

of a white boy, northern. of a Michigan leather.
of the white boy jacket, his leather like hair. The air is gray

like cig smoke. gray like ash. gray with the onset of northern
porchlike spring and its porchstep rain. wet

and snowy, the neighbor, his buddy in leather. like me, in leather.
In a wet snow, rocking. in a porchband leather. leather

in April. April wet and still, one foot to the other.

The day after *12 Years a Slave*

I make a stew. While one side of the landlord's futon gives out, the other

rests on one bolt. It all tips sideways and then

the mailman's footprints in snow.

The pot is on the stove,   but the meat is off.

   Do I throw out the meat. or eat the meat. The meat smells like a

slaughterhouse, it did. when it opened, a dead pigeon lies in a pan.

         blowflies.   the squeal of a small calf.

No one mentions the smell on their recipe blog. The snow

   piles windrift. one screw and then the other.

The maintenance man is suspicious of callers. also, I think, on heroin.

   Your control is out

            so be it, a fishsauce.   a splatter of thyme and cabbage.

The cat is a perched killer. the cutting board smeared parsley.

         (Northup had his own tune. choke sometimes. an ulcer of blear.

         I cry at the black rendering. the festival finish.

The chair squeals when I forget and fall on it. The house has it now.

It's all in the curtains. You cook until you have to give up and give in.
    A dutch oven keeps centuries' vapor.

        and a cow. what became of it. just to wind up in
        the trash.
            A starter. a hope for something right.

        I can see it there, marooned.

There was that breath on the caterpillar.
        It ruined the whole crop.

It is a Choice (because Kanye)

The rapper chooses his vacancies. Room does not
choose the rapper. The rapper walked into rooms. or
were dragged into rooms. were dragged
into rooms. Or we walked
into rooms. The seating charts of airplanes
look like the Middle Passage. Then we boarded the plane.
were dragged onto the plane. The plane
was dragged from us. Much like
the grocery store at night where in drag, the lights of we
dislocate. We remove ourselves from the store by
cuffed security. If we are a being,
then lightning has struck. We stand in the rain.
The lightning is big, the oppressive sky. It stood
us in wet. Between the door and between
the body, the mind is a temple at the end of his gun.
I brought my temple to his barrel in bliss.
His gun did flips. His gun was loving. He was
the kind of master who didn't trigger. We
was the body beneath all that. We, my body, got quite
beneath them. They dragged their bodies onto
mine. We opened all mouths to talk.
Genitals shackling, black over black in

                              the temple of take, the supine divinity.

                    The slaveship dance. The choice couldn't be, dear

prophet of rap, a choice against

monster or its poisoned tip. The slave

                              is a dance and a rope stood still, in its choice

                              of whip. its choice of lynch orifice to swallow

its sawed-off dick. Which pinkish meat

flesh, devour. Which exit to design, which

                              disemboweled master. A stand which

                              stood, was still or removed each larynx.

withstood machete each bludgeon become. To fight

with clarity is a kind of abstraction.

                              a tongue its cruelty. Eternal is choice.

                              To stand in a rage losing. We are

losing our democracy. Other people

decide what to do with their bodies. is a stand

                              to still until its pillage, and the laws

                              for long. But we choose, we

choose: if the sun is hot if the tulip

withers. We choose if the assault

                              is rifled, if the men come in stink.

                              We choose if the cum is drenching,

if the torture is daily. We choose

if the land the land is green and owned.

                              If the hunger, our stalkers.

                              our cops with fists. Whose

stalk is pushing back on lightning

the seasick air as it chooses to purge

                    the soggy wood of the hold,
                      and stay the enchained.

engorged white men rather
than reaching to the chokehold

                     and unscrewing
                    their sockets and filleting

their mouth. The water is coming
apart under our boats silt

                is useless. The body we submit
                   and stays and refuses

to give way. withstood
so could get dressed.

                 and choose what lingers
                   in order to get home.

what crawls in the muck.
what washed beneath in seawater.

Oregon Trail, Missouri

O trail up outta here, how long ago
     you started to wander, crawling milkweed
through dependence, in grope toward sprawl
dominion. Rather red in your rove from southern transition,

    thick of land use, what soft you carved of forest to get through
once dirt and fur and blood of original American and
bloody-scrape knuckles of emigrant pioneer. O what you woke
from sleep. dogwood drift loud and settling toward
expanse, like how a pride's breath

    can move blossom to shiver and roll over false aster, shape
border from its river source, return to river as fat pocketbook, mussel
of critical habit, long breather and muscular foot
under cypress and promise of tree. O path for packed wagon

    who dragged black slave alongside conduit, some salt
of new breeze, who swore deciduous freedom, and relented
only upon lawsuit in new land you opened to. O route
to burrow, you, like pipeline, leak the grease
of wayward stream. Trade off

and pick off growth in the way. How used, you. When
blue-promised god, some Negroes took up pack and white man's pack,
and given distance of black body to statehood pith, only made holy
states away. O what became you was over, the leaving grip bragged

all the way to the sea, already plundered and exhausted
of Shoshone patience and homesteading what hellbender
you've become. What uprooted clearing. stray cattle worth
whole encampments in fool's dust and deed. O what haven from man

who believe in America, only all to himself? Imagine

a way of shape that doesn't strangle. an arbor
of its very own leaf. Now, imagine
tern and piping plover that keeps expansion
        along its shore. a settlement for spring's deliver, not pipeline.

Imagine redbud staying put in its breeze and keeping us safely
strong as trees and dark as the bark of our open souls. Imagine
the park of evergreen surrender,
to a calmer, blue sky our govern might protect.

Imagine bald eagle again, not because white-headed
        but imagine bird, simple body of eager sea, talons
stretched over gold proportion. In summers, thick shiner.
In winter, undisturbed darter along somewhat snow, unstressed

by factory and loud humming fuel. O prairie of blazing star, imagine
full caves of left alone, unraided buffalo
clover, unhelped. unfringed orchid, unwestern. Imagine
    ground hallow, free to forage

its riverine root and plant vigor along the Missouri.

It Takes

The Eden the Negro shows the country boy poet, so she knows
the look in his eye. She knows the crook of his hat, how it stalls
in the mist night where fireflies and hissing crickets move
over fields. The Negro knows watching, how much standstill is twill
in prairie. Whatever brush between the star and dirt. She knows
lowland. tamp down and seed. What hunkers down between
the plush dander and the country poet's scythe. She has boots
without a sound to make. He has tree vision, the crawl of summer
bugs stuttering nameless. Unless the poet says *cicada*, think *locust*.
Unless a poet presses down a wing's sod to crush thorax
and antennae, think *hay*. Then the poet the Negro, the country
boy configure their horse and steady pistil behind standoff. Break
over pinball and dartboard and a bartender who makes bourbon
barrel in a bath where epithets infuse. How one might find a hick
in the dark, like a frog. like a white meat for bone and churn
in her mouth against the stark row of evening to pulp. Maybe
they want one another's head. They don't know the difference.
the growl insect and how stirred its body. as if blossom.
as if the ink creek of midnight speaks itself.

Forestbathing (*or* Trees)

for JW

Trees in other cities gather
and send out information. The beech,
the sylvatica, the Chinese birch judging

from the smell of diverted root.
I get more done with you in these curated woods.
Time now, is my humility. It scooches over

when we sit out under hydrangea, on a stone bench.
I trust you with the hammock and I lie beneath your
spiders in the wind. The Japanese garden is closed at this hour.

A group of teenagers gather with a chaperone and reach laughing
for wax bags they are told are full of squash sandwiches. There is always
another hill to climb and those kids were, all of them, brown.

One day I won't have to say how gravel gathers sun, but
today we mention its shutterframe. We talk about its dance in
orange petals. In this city, roads shoot up and we don't
park on them. We drive roundabout and try not
to think too slow.

Someone here in Boston always wants you
out of the way. But I remember the branch as it sways.
And I remember how much I have loved. And I remember
watching others light fire and wanting to get inside it.
And I want to ask, but don't

if then, were we more like trees, sending out seed signals
on a breeze. Reaching for each other in the dark where
it is cooler and want is damp. Or are we more like trees now.
Sedentary. Old and stock. Endangered and disbelieved.

My hair is falling out.

So give it to the midnight crows and let them bring it to
a little black girl should she set out seeds of a sunflower.
May they wrap it around a chip of bright amber or tuck
it inside the nostril of a rotting field mouse. Hide age.
Teach her meat, she needs to know. Though the pink tendon
is worse as we age. like a gate at which we like to shut our
eyes. Rub the sore scalp. Sleep to Liszt and catch a snail
which they like it's ok to make a world in which things
eat each other. Make room for believing. Climb down off
the world dying and feed something. Open up the yard.

That scene in *Killer of Sheep* when

she uses the dance to drape into
the circumference of a man. the quilt scale.
the rattle sprawl. the haunt absence
with its color gone. Too, her limbs

drag a revolve. The turn and a half it takes, it takes

a woman's whole life, having watched our mothers
want the peacock so bad, lament the parade.
the plume and the flaunt. His coming down
stairs in the morning. his pearl bead of sweat.

With iridescence, his jowl, as bitter earth ends
sore needle lifts and the bird never seemed to take

any grub she had to give.

Ablate the Suncups,
not the Ice: an Incantation

for L.

O god of the desublime, allay the vertical penitentes
their limbs, rest them back cold, not in precipitate
but in seed, in potential of hydrogen. Spoon in density

to be sung of their winter's seed and soak. Sip pond
to suncups, over sunrise. Far from the flat dispatch
of heat, its stench, its wayward ever summer barge

and fallout. Jesus be a river. Be a untainted float
of deliquescent surge. Be saltless and cold.
O pose of hope, allay the waterfall, hear their prayer,

O bed of oxygen, divine surge. Be also brackish sea. Be
seed of the frost, and supercooled. Be shade soup.
Sweet hale of beloved drench and mitochondrial belly,

be flint for the watery flame. Douse out the eventual
crunch, the big scorch, the rip of our primordial anus
and mouth, suckling at the place of eco abundance. O sweet bio teat,

O hygroscopic lordess. Were we to sit still and let ourselves be cold for hours, wiped of web crack frost, mild sud of the slow glacier, rimed vat at the edge of rash season, our legs from twitching.

O known keep of tomorrow, might we skill our motor by, pedal from the crib of our await. O stable evolver, an alms for safe passage, your earthen cooling, forgive us our erosion. Heal the demanding snows.

babysleep (drape)

her bodies belong the brown hobby.
stage every canvas. haunt the iris.
the backdrop says parlor. plies her flat
vaseline as stitched sea velvet, as
baby's soft, oiled cheek. the viewer's
opaque fail. tumid and hip, the weave's
dazzle mantled wall and cloistered night
sun like women, black and lipstick. be
kept from. semantic, switch of lovegrass
black and apple, flung stars in heavy
sienna dust night, burning like hot
comb temple altar and kneeling night
host, assembled into body's stock.

Curtains

Whose held belly at center she frame. Situs poised true
in situ. The Africanist of glimmer gaze upon
dark nations in return. The sifter, supplants glitter.
oiled and brandish, rouge and lippish, fetish and brogue, thick
lipstick, swole blue hip, the wish and the aureole, the
saddle and the want nipple, the ones high priestess doing
a high thigh curtain, unlashed in soft netting, unleashed
in that poppin' hair, or that grassy flat, gods beginning.
or not so Venus, sung to the oblong glare, women
mustering, a host of sistren, the host of our lost black
semantic doubles over heavy sienna. It's
the viewer's failure to weave and dazzle at artifice.
in lust with hot comb burn and altar kneeled to the back
at home temple. Us like a body in a stocking, some

after Deana Lawson

days, lip o' lovely in rainbow crotch shot. How I love
her stung blue sofa, crouched and ejaculating hifi
hydrant sprung from childhood's articulate couch. Father
disrobed and hung like a thoroughly dented drape, against
the dismantled, fussy mother and burnt afterbirth
spilling along the interior lawn hosed and shiny
and thus diluted melanin sibling packaged in
blackgrass and star apple and flung one side of the fawn room
to the next. what black women be kept from. that loom look
haunting the iris. hurled into the flat black of baby
sleep, the intentional length goes on among infants'
witness, from the rhythm of tone in a sister's hip. her
lovers dressed inside huge tits. the sag coo you amply
finger. the radiators hissing up the thin, sheer seams.

(drape) sleepbaby

through days spent between body, and so
midlove in the hydrant sprung of green
living, an articulation of
sex and notice, whose father's grass makes
humus earth, genetic. in other
words, some gods begin in a sleep swing
grassy infants, marked by netting of
bush; that poppin' hair; wombs of couple
fucking. the splendid melanin of
dirt soil, drench planets, brandish and rogue
rouge and lippish, rough witness behind
curtained lash, the birth of lovers dressed
easily soft inside black's huge tits.

Self-Portrait as Good Samaritan

It's been long enough ago hasn't it, wherein we used to call cops
on a woman gathering her too-skinny boy by the coat collar let
the system work it out tell the cops come get this woman before I put
my hands on her all the while her boy just moaning so soft what it could

mean if I did. or what else to do the same as it always meant truth be
told I am in a warm café and reading Zora by near candlelight and earth
wind and fire on the speakers and the sound is mellow and I am just
happy how smart she is which took us so long to know how much

Oluale Kossola takes the Affica route and she hears it all and writes it
all down and if I was a filmmaker I'd make that script for Tiffany
Haddish I don't know who would play Cudjo Lewis, but I know Zora
was funny and wild and big-voiced and didn't stay too long on any

given point she was already done with and there is a photo of Cudjo
and his two precious grandbabies that he picked out those perfect
peaches from a bin of fresh picked peaches and gave them to the
grandbabies so they could run and go play and Jericho is right in saying

now if I put a perfect peach in a poem it somehow mean I am thinking
of Ross Gay and I try to think if I would be a patient mother or if I
would be the woman whose boy other people want to take away or
at least get him out my house for a while I don't keep

people too close for long before they figure out I can be cold not cruel
but I can snap and my moods I guess I get from my mother that I don't
much like it when people gauge my personality like they would know for
me it's easier if when my roommate tells me the story of a woman

on the train who was cussing out her baby boy and when she went
to put her hands on him her friend said *fight me instead* and she did
she tried but evidently that didn't work out because her friend put that
woman in a hospital and still it seem like that's better than calling

the cops on her now but it's always been that way ain't it Zora Neale
Hurston asked Cudjo to tell her about being the last living man
who knew and so Kossola told her stories about the village in which
his grandfather led the path of a king only for the king to order the head

of a man who took a whisker from a lion's jowl meant for the king
to be taken off after the love is gone is off then it's billy jean and fine
but then it's thriller and then the way you make me feel and I don't
understand but I'm shaking and no one is saying any thing so I do

go up to the counter and ask *what's with the run* it's kind of tone deaf
and she says I can change it and I do. do that and she does. change it.

———

In "*Limulus Polyphemus*" the italicized text is taken from the Wikipedia entry of the same name, commonly known as the horseshoe crab.

"Against Storm, Against Glib Thunder" is written after a poem of similar structure by Timothy Donnelly.

"*Language works over information . . .*" takes its title and some italicized lines from remembered exchanges between Ron Silliman and audience members during his lecture at Wayne State University, 2007. These may or may not be direct quotes.

"Sonata in F Minor, K.183: Allegro" makes reference to *The Street*, the classic 1946 novel by Ann Petry.

"So is we thinking up new ways to fuck, or nah." is a phonetic remix of Ty Dolla $ign's "Or Nah" featuring The Weeknd. One sentence is retained from the original.

"It Takes" is written after Frank Stanford's poem "The Brake."

ACKNOWLEDGMENTS

Thank you, Kaveh Akbar, Laylah Ali, Jericho Brown, Andre Cobb, Melissa Crowe, Alex Dimitrov, Timothy Donnelly, Tarfia Faizullah, Ross Gay, Duriel E. Harris, Niki Herd, A. Van Jordan, Shayla Lawson, Dana Levin, Dawn Lundy Martin, Philip Matthews, Gregory Pardlo, Jana Prikryl, Justin Phillip Reed, Don Share, Marcus Wicker, and Lisa Williams, for your love, friendship, editorial considerations and inclusions, mentorship, and support.

Thank you, Carl Phillips, for your encouragement on this collection and your immensely helpful suggestions.

Thank you, Jonathan Galassi, for your stellar eye, and for your confidence in this work.

I am incredibly thankful to the following institutions, which have offered financial support and time to write over the past several years:

National Writers Series in Traverse City, Michigan

MacDowell Colony

Creative writing program at Washington University in St. Louis

Dorothy and Lewis B. Cullman Center for Scholars and Writers at the New York Public Library

Helen Zell Writers' Program at the University of Michigan

These poems first appeared, sometimes in different form, in the following publications:

Academy of American Poets: "Single Lines Looking Forward *or* One Monostich Past 45" and "Oregon Trail, Missouri." "The Neighbor's Buddy Through the Window" also appeared under a slightly different title.

The American Poetry Review: "Ablate the Suncups, not the Ice: an Incantation," "Self-Portrait as Good Samaritan," and "*Limulus Polyphemus*"

Beloit Poetry Journal: "Versal"

Berkeley Poetry Review: "She is what I undo"

Boston Review: "Reflections in a Pool of Hair," "What Milkman Leaps For," "The fat of the fog hovers over," and "It Takes"

The Cortland Review: "Abortion"

Heavy Feather Review: "Stand Up" (subsequently withdrawn from its archive)

Indiana Review: "Here is the sweet hand you always turn back on yourself"

The New Republic: "My hair is falling out."

The New York Review of Books: "It is a Choice (because Kanye)" and "Sonata in F Minor, K.183: Allegro"

PEN Poetry Series: "Against Storm, Against Glib Thunder," "Anise Swallowtail, Molting," and "White People Eating White Food"

POETRY: "Curtains"

Spoon River Poetry Review: "The day after *12 Years a Slave*"